# CHOCOLATE &

# VANILLA

## A RECIPE FOR A HAPPY LIFE

By
Cheryl Gillespie

# DEDICATION

There are many people in my life who have given me guidance and inspiration in the development of this beautiful book. I would like to thank all of you who have shared an experience with me. I appreciate you and my lessons.

First and foremost, my beautiful daughter Melissa, who has taught me how beautiful, amazing, and precious life is. She taught me all about pure love and joy, and with her, I have had the courage and strength to move forward in my life. She is a true blessing to me and all who come in contact with her.

To my beautiful friends Pamala and Terry, who knew I was writing this book and helped me keep it a secret until it was finished. Their friendship and encouragement mean the world to me. To my dear friends Tony, Kathy, Donna, Nancy, Mary Jo, Remi,

Odette, Kathy, and Carrie, who helped me see conflict and taught me that you can still be friends even if you do have differences of opinion. To my friend Troy, who is always there for me. Lily, my friend, and inspiration who introduced me to Abraham.

To my mom, who has been there for me through it all. She has taught me to be strong in any situation. I am thankful she gave me the space in which I was able to write this book. I love and appreciate you, Mom, for who you are and all you do. And to my siblings, Louie, Jackie, and Pauline, thank you for who you are. You have taught me to be happy in adversity, even though we have our own thoughts on a subject. Throughout our upbringing, I have learned that even though we were raised the same way in the same house, we are all different and shine our love. Thank you! I love you!

# ACKNOWLEDGMENTS

Through the passions and teaching of others, I have learned so much!

I am thankful for Louise Hay, Ester, and Jerry Hicks, and Dr. Wayne Dyer, just to name a few.

There is Gary Young of Young Living Oils who has been such an inspiration in my life. Along with Peter Gleim of Bemer Internation.

# CONTENTS

**CHAPTER 1** Chocolate and Vanilla... Find Your Flavor.......................... 1

**CHAPTER 2** Viewpoints and Belief Systems ........................................ 12

**CHAPTER 3** Mood and Alignment...................................................... 20

**CHAPTER 4** What We Attract ............................................................ 31

**CHAPTER 5** How Can We Be of Service to Others............................... 44

**CHAPTER 6** Influenced by Other Viewpoints..................................... 57

**CHAPTER 7** Interpretation of A Viewpoint ........................................ 65

**CHAPTER 8** How Do You Feel About It?............................................. 78

**CHAPTER 9** How to Stay in Alignment .............................................. 84

**CHAPTER 10** Who Are You? .............................................................. 95

**ABOUT THE AUTHOR** ....................................................................106

**REFERENCES** ................................................................................107

# CHAPTER 1

## Chocolate and Vanilla... Find Your Flavor

To find your flavor, you must know what that is. Chocolate and Vanilla, as I always say, can mean completely different things to different people. It is all in the interpretation and the belief system. I have used this term for as long as I can remember. For me, it means a difference of opinion. I like Chocolate, and you like Vanilla. So instead of saying opinions are like assholes, and we all have one. I choose to say, "Chocolate and Vanilla". Of course, there are a couple hundred flavors, just like our opinions. I just found that when conversing with someone, this was a more polite way of saying, you have your opinion, and I have mine, and we are both correct.

Since I was a young girl, I always saw things in a different light. I noticed that I viewed things much differently than my siblings and my friends. I would always see the brightness and the positive in others. I would try and find the good in any situation around me. Whereas others would be mad or fearful looking at the negative. I could somehow tune into others. I would know how they were feeling without talking with them. I would do my best to stay away from the negative and walk towards the positive. I guess you could say I like a little flavor in my life, and I would look for that in everyone. I like colorful, bright, shiny things. In essence, my filter would always be bright and flavorful. So why relate life situations to Chocolate and Vanilla? Well, to me Vanilla is delicious and plain and clean, but Chocolate is scrumptious and decatenate and interesting. They are complete opposites, yet they are the same. Whatever it is, icecream, cake, or even a protein shake, it is the same yet different flavors. Some would say well, that is just black and white big deal. Yes, it is, but it's how you look at it. Is the glass half empty or half full? Some would say it is refillable! How do you perceive that? What filter are you using? What is your interpretation? What is your viewpoint?

Many things are black and white. Like, this paper is white with black ink, very basic. What if I was to add some color to it? Maybe green or blue writing. As you know, there are many colors in the rainbow. And these colors can be mixed to make more colors. Scientists estimate that there are about 10 million colors in the world. Yet there are only 7 colors in the rainbow. Wow, how is that possible? I believe that in the mixing of those 7 colors, we can make multiple colors. For that to have happened someone had to try it. Someone came up with the idea of wanting more colors, and they experimented. Try it, take some paint, chalk, pencils or markers. Just start with 2 colors and mix them. For instance, if you take blue and red, what do you get? Purple, right, and if you mix yellow and blue, you get green. Can you make white or is it just bleached or has some type of additive in it? Is it just there? You can mix a bunch of colors together and just keep adding until, eventually, you will get black. Something you learned in kindergarten, right? So why the color lesson here? If you can just stay with me a bit, you will see the connection to your flavor or, as I call it, your filter and interpretation of life.

I want to build on what you already know. See, mixing colors is like mixing opinions, flavors, filters, interpretations or understanding. Remember, opinions are like assholes, everyone has one. We have more than one opinion. So, maybe I will relate it to something other than body parts. And that's where your filter comes in.

Some people see life in black and white. It is either right or wrong, rich or poor, big or small. Then you have others who see a colorful life like maybe a lesson or experience, freedom or independence, medium or different sizes. We all interpret life differently. Sometimes, it's nice to mix things up. Look at it from a different viewpoint. Take a little from here and a little from there and mix it up, add it to what I like.

Let's go back to Chocolate and Vanilla for a bit. In remembering what happened when we mixed colors together. What do you think when we mix flavors together? Exactly, we get different flavors. Can you remember a time you experimented and mixed two flavors together? What was it? Maybe Chocolate and peanut butter or Vanilla and caramel. Or maybe you think outside of the box and mix them all together. Whatever it is, I'm sure at some point in your life, you have played around with different flavors in your ice cream. Maybe even add a little crunch, and maybe you like it just the way it is.

Now let's take your everyday food. What do you like? Are you a meat eater (translation: carnivore)? Or maybe you are a plant-based eater (translation: vegetarian). How about someone who doesn't eat eggs, dairy, or meat (translation: vegan). Whatever it is you like is awesome! Something you enjoy. Think of it as your flavor. Now, if you are a vegetarian, have you ever sat across the table for a meal with a meat eater? I am sure at some point in your life, this has happened. Well, how was that meal for you? How did it make you feel? What was going through your mind when they were eating the one thing you despised? Did you say something to them? Did you choke? Did you get up from the table? Were you dismissive of them and leave? Did you give them a rundown on what they were eating?

If this was a business meal, chances are that you politely sat there eating your salad, trying to focus on the person you were with, not their meal. If it was a family member, you may not have been so nice and said what you were thinking.

Now, Let's break this down. Is it wrong for the other person to eat meat because you are a vegetarian? Or maybe it's wrong for you to eat a salad because they are carnivores? No, No! It's not wrong for either of you. You are different people with different dietary needs. You both must eat food for nourishment. You just like different types of food. You both have a different flavor for food and life! You see things from a different perspective, Chocolate and Vanilla! You understand this and that is why you can sit across the table enjoying each other's company and a meal. It's ok!!! It's ok to be different, it's ok to have your own opinion! It's ok to have your own flavor! It's okay to be you! We all get to express our individuality.

Now, what would transpire if you were to try and see someone else's viewpoint. Like seeing that meal for what it was, nourishment. What would happen if you were to ask questions about it. Maybe, why do you eat what you eat? What is it about that meal that you like? How does it taste? Explain it to me. Do you think you would understand how meat would taste? Or the salad? I wonder if you can taste something using just your opinion. Can you taste it with your vision? Maybe you can taste it with your thoughts? You see, the only way to really know what the food tastes like is to taste it. Just like you must put your hand on the stove to know that the stove is hot.

Have you ever tried to explain to someone what chocolate cake tastes like? What about Vanilla ice cream? They really must taste it to get the flavor.

So, when I talk about Chocolate and Vanilla it's my filter, my flavor to help me get my point across. Why do I use this analogy? Because most people know of or have tried Chocolate and or Vanilla at some point in their life. Now I know there are many different flavors like Mint chocolate, salted caramel, cookies and cream, and strawberry. They say about 1,000 different flavors. But this is simple to understand and just because I like Chocolate and you like Vanilla, it doesn't make it wrong. We both like what we like, and that is ok! We love what we love. We all have our flavor! Whatever flavor that is, it's perfect for each one of us.

Is there a flavor that brings you joy? When you think of it, do you smile, get excited, and start to salivate? Is it ice cream, candy, cake, or something sweet or salty? What about the way you view life? Does it feel the same? Do you get excited each day to be living the life you are living? Do you do what makes you happy? Is life sweet or salty for you? If you live at the beach, it can be both!

Remember, everyone's interpretation is different. It depends on the vibration you are on. Have you ever been out with a friend or family member in the same place but had two totally different experiences? You had a great time where the other person did not.

I have had many experiences like this. Whether it was at someone's house, in a restaurant, or even traveling or going to a concert or sporting event. Let's take, for instance, going to a hockey game. You are both in the same place, sitting next to each other. A large arena it's cold, full of excitement and crazy fans. Maybe you have a cold drink, and your friend has a hot drink. You may be full of joy and excitement because you love hockey and your favorite team is playing. Your friend may love hockey also, but it is not their favorite team. You both are having the same experience, but your friend is not having a good time. You, on the other hand, can't contain your excitement. You are cheering them on, jumping for joy. Your team is winning! You look at your friend with joy and happiness, and there they are, sitting like a lump. But wait, how can that be? I thought, *you loved hockey? Why are you so unhappy? What's going on with you?* Well, you see, even though you are in the same place doing the same thing and having the same experience, you are filtering it differently. You are taking it all in through the lens you are looking out of. You are excited to be there and are happy, but your friend is sad and not happy like you are to be there. Maybe because their team is not involved in the game, and they do not know who to root for. Maybe they received some bad news earlier that day. Maybe they are just cold and don't want to be involved. Maybe they are just not present in the moment. Whatever it is, they are filtering their experience through their interpretation as you are yours. Different flavors for different people. Does that make it wrong or even right? Just like reading this book. Each person will interpret it differently.

Can two or more people have the same experience and be right? It's just a different viewpoint. We all see life through our own lens. We have our own belief systems. Remember, we said opinions are like assholes. We all have one. Well, our viewpoints are just that. Our belief systems create our perspectives and opinions, which will translate into emotions, and that is how we get through this thing we call life. We feel our way. If something doesn't feel good, we do not continue to do it. If it feels good, we do.

# CHAPTER 2

## Viewpoints and Belief Systems

Where do we get our viewpoints from? How did we develop this belief system? Why do I have a different belief than others around me? I even have a different viewpoint than my siblings. Yet I grew up in the same house with the same parents.

Let's explore this a bit. What is a belief system? Belief is a thought you keep thinking. It is the way we look at life and the way we digest it. Have you ever heard the term looking through rose-colored glasses? You probably have heard that term many times in your life. Most times people say that to another when they think they are so happy or positive. They may say one is delusional. Mostly because the one using the term is in a very different place. They are not happy or positive.

They are on the opposite side of the stick. Which would be unhappy or negative. Same stick with two ends on opposite sides. Very different viewpoints or perhaps different lenses.

Someone who is positive will always see the glass as half full. Someone who is negative will see it as half-empty. Someone who has a creative mind will see that glass as refillable. So, tell me, is there a right or wrong answer here. It is our interpretation through our thoughts and feelings, and we are all right for ourselves. Whichever way we look at something, it is right for the person looking. Remember the two people at the hockey game. Well, the excited one walked into that game with that happy, excited attitude, and their experience was such. You may say they had on their rose-colored glasses. The other person was down and unhappy, and when entering the room, they viewed it with that lower energy. Shall we say with grey glasses? Can you understand how two people could be at the same place at the same time and have two very different experiences? They will talk about it the way they view it. If you were to ask each one of them, how was the game? They would tell you based on the way they viewed it.

In essence, we are talking about opposites. Happy and sad, positive and negative, Rose and Grey. Same stick, two different sides. So, the answer is yes, two people can be in the same place at the same time doing the same thing, having two different experiences. This is what I refer to as Chocolate and Vanilla.

We are all spirit in a physical body. We are all the same, but you see, we all have our own operating system, and depending on what we download into it is what will shine through.

Our bodies are like that. I am sure you have heard at some point in your life the saying. If you put good in, you will get good out. If you put junk in, junk will come out, just like our diets. If you eat bad food, you will feel bad. If you eat good food, you will feel good. Our minds and Spirit are the same. It's all in what you feed your mind, body, and spirit. It's all about alignment.

When you are in alignment, you feel happy or peaceful. You will then see things through those rose-colored glasses. When you are out of alignment you are grouchy or crabby, you will have on the grey colored ones.

We talked about how you see things. Your looking glass or viewpoint, shall we say. Listed below are just a few things that we see and or do differently from others.

The famous view of......

Is it gravy or sauce?

Toilet paper roll, should it be over or under?

Window blinds, should they close in or out?

Washing dishes, sponge, or wash cloth?

Paper towels or cloth towels?

Shower curtains inside or outside the tub?

Paper or plastic?

Folding the laundry.

House temperature, hot or cold?

Parking in the garage, head or tail in?

Food sweet or spicy?

Chocolate or Vanilla?

Starting to get the picture? Ask yourself this question, does it really matter? Is any of this important to who I am? What kind of person do I want to be? Will any of this help me?

Maybe.... Maybe not. Always two sides to every coin, but there are many sides to an opinion. Each side is our point of view. There are billions of people in the world having their view of things. We have all been conditioned to believe things in a certain way. Have you ever heard that there are about 270 ways to wash dishes? Do I like a sponge or a cloth, drainboard on the right or left? Do I fill the sink with water? Do I just leave the dishes in the sink and load the dishwasher later? How were you taught to wash the dishes? Is any of this the wrong way? No, it is all in what you prefer. So, when I asked if it really matters. What did you answer?

Either way, you are correct. It is your preference to wash your dishes the way you like. What matters is your viewpoint for you and how you view your life. Do any of these things make you happy? If they do, keep doing them. If not, stop!

What you do and how you do it matters to you. You would not go into your friend or family member's house and tell them they are doing it wrong, would you? Maybe you would, and if that is the case, just stop. It is not your business how they wash their dishes or fold their laundry. You don't live there, and it does not affect you! After all, would you want them to come into your home and tell you, *you have it all wrong*, that they do it this way and their way is right. I doubt it. So just remember there are many ways to wash dishes, and it is not your sink and not your dishes!

Be conscious of what you give out because you will get in return. You project what you feel. If you really feel someone is doing something that will hurt them. Just be gentle and let them know it's just your opinion.

Here is a cute story with an interesting viewpoint.

There were four generations of women preparing a holiday dinner. They have all learned how to prepare these special dinners from their mother. The youngest of the generations was just learning and was very inquisitive.

She asked her mother, "Mom, why do you cut the ham and put it in the pot?"

Her Mom replied, "I don't know. That's how my mom did it. It's a good question. How about you go and ask Grandma."

"Grandma, why do you cut the ham before you put it in the pot?"

"Well, darling, this is the way my mom taught me to cook it."

"Ok, what is the reason for cutting the ham before it goes into the pot. Does it cook better?" asked the little girl.

"Darling, I do not have the answer. Go and ask my mom this question."

So, the little girl went into the dining room and asked her great-grandmother. "Grandmother, can you please tell me why you cut the ham before you put it in the pot? I asked Mother and Grandma, and neither knew the answer."

She said, "That's simple. When I was growing up and first started cooking, I didn't have a pot big enough. So, I had to cut the ham in half for it to fit."

And so all three generations believed that they had to cut the ham before putting it in the pot.

# CHAPTER 3

## Mood and Alignment

How did you feel when you woke up this morning? Were you rested or feeling groggy? Did you feel excited to start your day, or did you want to go back to sleep and spend your day in bed with your sheets over your head? Did you do anything to be in a better place for yourself? How did you start your day, breakfast, coffee, a run or a walk with the dog? Maybe you had to get your kids to school or even rush off to work. Rushing around and couldn't get it all done. How did your mood carry over into the day? Let's see: If you were out of alignment or unhappy, I bet you forgot your keys, dropped your coffee, forgot your lunch, or maybe got stuck in traffic, and the day continued in that energy from there. Now, imagine if you were in alignment or happy. How different would that day have gone? You would have your keys with you. Coffee and lunch in hand and navigated traffic like a champ! Get into work with a smile on your face because you got to work before your coworkers. They were stuck in all that traffic. Your day had a beautiful flow to it, where you felt at ease just moving from one thing to another. Nothing seemed to bother you.

Can you see the difference between being in and out of alignment? Here is another example. Think about a time in your life when you were so happy. It could be when you were a young kid at Christmas time. Maybe a time in High school with your friends. Maybe that special person showed up in your life. Maybe you got married. Maybe had a child. Maybe you bought a new car. Maybe you hit a goal you were working on. Maybe you won the lottery. Whatever that happy time was for you. I want you to remember it. Now, think back to how you felt at that time. Happy, excited, joyful, loving.... There are many words to describe how you felt, and at that time, you were in alignment. With that feeling in mind, what would happen if your boss, parent, teacher, child, sibling, or partner asked you to do something you didn't like to do or asked you for something they wanted. You would be agreeable, and it probably would not have been a problem for you. You probably would have said sure, my pleasure. Now think about a time that you were angry in your life. Nothing was going the way you wanted it to. You had one challenge after another.

Describe that feeling: maybe bad-tempered, angry, sad, frustrated, in a bad mood. Again, many words to describe how you felt at that time. That is what we call out of alignment. Now, go back to that same person with that same request. How would you respond to that? Most likely, you would say no and leave me alone. Or whatever else you thought of. Why is that? It is the same person with the same request. You were just in a bad mood at the time of the request. This is the difference between being in alignment and out of alignment. When in alignment, you are happy to give, do, and go along with the situation. But when you are out of alignment, watch out!

There is pushback, resistance, and frustration. Why do we do this to ourselves? Didn't it feel much better to be in alignment and happy than out of alignment and angry? We get more out of our lives when we are happy. When we put on those rose-colored glasses, we see things in beauty and abundance. My dad used to always say you can catch more bees with honey than vinegar.

**Alignment:** What is it, and how do we achieve it?

I find alignment is like your barometer. When you're hot, you're hot, and when you're cold, you're cold. When there is balance, there is peace.

You see, whether we translate things in flavor; chocolate or vanilla, color; rose or grey, or temperature; hot or cold. It just shows us how we are feeling at that very moment. And how we feel is the most important viewpoint we can have. Our emotions guide us.

Have you ever had a good friend who you did everything with? You talked on the phone, telling them everything. When you had a bad day, you would call them and complain about it. When you had a good day, you would share with them. They would probably do the same. And when you had an important decision to make you would call and run it by them. Maybe you want to change jobs, and you need some help in making that decision. You wanted your best friend's guidance and opinion. After all they know you best and would never steer you wrong. You had the conversation with your friend, and their response was: I would just say stay where you are. It's comfortable; you have been there for a long time, and you know you can survive on your salary. You are comfortable with your co-workers. Yet, in your mind, you thought all of that was boring. I want a change, something new and exciting. I want to meet new people, and I want to be challenged to make more money. Same details two different viewpoints. You were a bit conflicted, but you decided to listen to your friends' advice because what if they were right.

What if I took the other job and I was unhappy or couldn't make it work. Their opinion made you nervous. So, you passed up the opportunity that was given to you and decided to stay put in this job where you weren't going anywhere but were stable and comfortable. Even though you weren't happy. But as time went on day to day you just got by. You were bored but stable. You still wondered, but what if? What if I took that other opportunity? Where would I be? Then you talked about it with your friend again and again. Continuously complaining about it and growing more unhappy. Then you started to resent your friend for your decision. Ultimately, it was your decision. They just gave you advice based on their own feelings, their barometer at that time. We cannot be mad at someone else because we listened to their advice. It would be like picking up the hot coal to throw at them, but you are the one being burned. Remember, you can ask 100 people for their opinion, and you will get 100 different answers.

Everyone goes through life at their own pace with their own choices. Everything we do is a choice. Even if we do not choose, the choice will be made for us. No answer is the answer. The point is that how we feel at that very moment is how we will view things. That doesn't mean you chose the wrong thing. It just means that you choose based on how you felt at that time. So, choose to feel good, and you will choose what is best for you. I find that when I'm in a bad place and make a decision, it doesn't always turn out to be the best for me.

When I was learning about emotions and feelings and how they related to my decisions in life. I would always experiment. I had to put these things to the test. My ego was ruling at that time. I was learning a lot about my food choices. So here is something I experimented with. An apple and a slice of pizza. Now, I was always told that an apple is one of the healthiest foods you can eat and that pizza was fattening. I didn't necessarily agree with that. Of course, I love pizza and thought it has tomato sauce (Veggie), cheese (protein), and dough (carb). I thought and still do think pizza is a balanced food for me to eat. It's just yummy! On the other hand, an apple, one of life's sweetest treats, was good too. Just different.

With that being said, I had been going through some difficulties in my life. With a lot of crazy, depressing emotions, I had been experiencing, and my body reflected this. I had gained a lot of weight, and most of the foods I was eating affected my body in a way that I would not feel well. I had some intense digestive issues. I started seeing a holistic chiropractor who was a kinesiologist. This person tested my body for many different types of food. For a period of time, I had to eliminate so much food from my diet that, at one point, I was only eating lettuce, cucumbers, string beans, zucchini, and apples. Everything else would just bother my system. This went on for some time. I did lose a lot of weight and started feeling better. But noticed that when I was in a bad mood whatever I ate just bothered me. This is where the experiment came in.

I was reading Louise Hay's book "You Can Heal Your Life." Today, this book is like my Bible. I started to experiment with my emotions and my eating habits. I noticed that when I was out with friends, enjoying myself having a meal with them, I felt good. I tried a food that was on the bad list at that point, and I noticed I was fine and it didn't have any effect on me. Later that week I had a bad day at work, and I grabbed an apple. My thoughts were, *well, I can grab the chocolate that is here, or the apple.* Because you know an apple is a much better choice than chocolate, so I'm told. I ate that apple, but the funny thing about it was it made me sick. I could not digest it. That seemed to be the issue with me along. I could not digest my food, and it made me sick. I grabbed my book and looked up the body part or the problem.

Alongside the problem are two statements. One states the probable cause, and the other new thought pattern. So, I worked on this and repeated the new thought pattern. It really seemed to help.

At this point in my life, I was going through many changes in my relationships and my work. I wanted to just be free of it all. I decided it was time for me to get out and enjoy my life a little. I called a friend; she was also going through her junk. We decided to hit the clubs like we did when we were younger. From then on, just about every weekend, my girlfriend and I would go out dancing. We had a ball! We danced and laughed without a care in the world. We met and talked with new people and just had so much fun. For us, dancing was like exercising but gave us that free feeling. One night, after all this fun, we decided to grab a slice of pizza. Yes, at that time in my life, we had late-night food available to us. We could go to a diner or a pizza place after hours. Ah, the good old days. Remember, I was on this pretty strict diet at the time, and I hadn't had pizza in over 1.5 years! Yeah, I couldn't believe it either. I'm Italian, we ate pizza for breakfast and dinner. Well, I made the decision to eat just one piece, and boy, was that delicious!

The best I had ever had! To my surprise, I felt light no discomfort like in the past. What was happening? I felt so good that I ate a second slice! Oh, these slices were double the regular sizes, but it was so good! I was in such joy and so excited to eat this food that my body never felt the pizza. Quite different than what I felt when I ate that apple in despair. What I am saying is that it is all about how you feel. Everything in life is how you feel. When you feel good, you are good. That was the same pizzeria I have been going to for years. The same recipe of pizza that in the past made me sick. Safe to say it had nothing to do with the pizza. It was me. It was the vibration I was on each time that determined how I digested my food.

When you change the way you view something, what you view changes. It's all in how you look at it. It is ok that some days we have on grey glasses, but we can quickly put on rose-colored ones. Once we know how to change our vibration.

# CHAPTER 4

## What We Attract

Let's talk about a saying 'like attracts like.' Somehow, I always knew if I liked something that I was doing I would be happy. But what I didn't know is that how I felt at a particular time would bring more of the same to me. My emotions are like looking in a mirror, reflecting back to me where I am at any given moment in time.

Remember your friend you always talked with. Did you ever notice if you were complaining about something, more of the same would show up during your day? You probably asked yourself why is this happening to me? I am a good person. What is with all this negative stuff happening? Well, like attracts like. That goes for everything in this world. The rich get richer, the sick get sicker, etc., etc. It took me some time to really get this.

I am a positive and happy person. I would help wherever I could. I would volunteer in a church or school. When I was out, I was always courteous to others. You know the drill. So why did I have other issues? Like my relationships. I am sure you have questioned yourself at some point in your life. Funny how we question ourselves when things are not going the way we want them to. When it all goes well we just enjoy without question.

One day, I just realized that if I felt good and was happy, nothing bothered me. I would give my daughter anything she wanted. I would help everyone, and I was able to achieve a lot. But if I was in a bad mood, everything bothered me. I did nothing to help others, and everything went array. Have you ever experienced this?

I was not a particularly good student at that time of my life. You really couldn't tell me anything. I was cranky and short with others. I was trying to be positive, but really, any little thing would set me off. I showed I was happy on the outside, but on the inside, I was miserable. I was looking for something to help myself. I purchased one book after another. I did have a lot of good books, and I would just look at them sitting on the shelf. As if by looking at them, I would know what they were all about. You know, magically, I would be healed. I decided to just grab one off the shelf and flip it to a page. I read something like if you change the way you look at something, what you look at will change. Although that took some time to sink in. Like what does that mean? If I turn my head to the side, it will straighten out. Maybe I have to stand on my head, not my feet. LOL!! I finally got it. Change your damn attitude. Change your viewpoint, change your filter. Even then, my attitude was of a know-it-all.

You see, I had a particular way of doing things. And when it came to raising my daughter and my household, well... no one could tell me how to or even try to do it for me. It was my way, and I was right!! I had no idea that there were so many opinions then. So many ways to do things. Looking back, it was right for me at that time. It was the way I went about it that brought so much stress and anxiety to my life. My vibration as such was low, and that like-attracts-like thing was working.

This saying, "Change the way you look at it, and it will change," I learned from Dr. Wayne Dyer. This man has eight children. Eight children! He was so calm and confident. I only had one and was a banshee, you know, like a crazy person. I did take everything on myself. I was raising my daughter, volunteering at school, Girl Scout leader, teaching CCD, volunteering at church, cooking, cleaning, laundry, working with my husband at our Chicken Holiday, working on my business, and had two dogs, having holidays at our house for 20 people or so. You know what that entails; planning, shopping, cooking, cleaning, and entertaining.

What the hell was I thinking? Apparently, I wasn't. I just took it all on myself and did it all. Like I was going to get some great prize or something. This is what I learned from my mother. No, I didn't accept any help. That's because it had to be my way. I didn't realize it at the time. I later found out this was an old conditioning I was raised with. There is only one way, and if I did not do it that way, I was not good enough. Nothing was ever good enough. Something Dr. Dyer said in that book hit me. I am good enough!! I just do things a different way. I do them my way. As I repeated this to myself over and over. I am enough. I am enough. I started to soften, not a lot, but just enough to realize I was not happy and became resentful. That was a very low vibration and a challenging time in my life.

I always knew the golden rule of treating others the way you want to be treated. I did follow that premise, so what was happening here? I treated others better than myself. I learned that it is good to treat others with love, kindness, and respect. I also learned that you cannot pour from an empty cup. And that is what was happening to me. I was empty. I gave and gave until I had nothing left to give. So, how did I get here, and what do I do about it. And what does this have to do with Chocolate and Vanilla and this book?

We all have a process to go through here on earth. We have the experience of living life and have lessons to learn during this life. We have a purpose here: to love, learn, and grow. And as we do that, we can help others. We help others in many ways. You may have heard the saying, "You must put your hand on the stove to know the stove is hot. Or, if you want to get to the other side of a minefield, do you blaze your own trail or follow the footsteps of the person who did it successfully?"

I tried to do my own thing. While some of it was working the other part was not. So, I found others to help me. I read books and attended seminars. I went to counseling. I was told I needed a break. I read that being in nature helps to ground you. Even if just sitting in nature. I always loved being outside. But I didn't know how to be still. I had to be busy, so I tried gardening and spending more time with my dogs outside in winter, spring, summer, and fall. My daughter loved it also. Still busy, but being outside had a more calming effect on me.

I can remember a time when we spent a lot of time outside, playing, planting, and swimming. I noticed I felt a lot better and happier when I was out in nature with the sun. One day, my daughter was out with her dad. I was outside gardening. I went inside through our large sliding glass doors, and as soon as I went to close the door, a very large frog was there. I had closed the door on him. Oh my God!! I freaked out! What did I do?! My dogs were barking, and I started screaming as though the house was on fire! My daughter and her dad were just pulling into the driveway and heard the commotion. They came running in to see what was going on. I was so loud that they could hear me outside. What is it? Are you ok?! There I was, standing away from the door, looking at that poor frog trying to keep my dogs away. My daughter ten at the time, ran right to it. Opened the door and picked it up and cradled him. She started crying. What did you do to him? Now

I'm good with dogs and cats but frogs? No, thank you! She is standing there with this very large frog in her hand, crying. I was squeamish, and my husband was laughing, and the dogs were running around. It was crazy. Three different people with three different experiences and feelings in the same situation. To say we all reacted differently is an understatement. My daughter looked at that frog with such love and compassion. I looked at it as slimy, and it didn't belong in my house, but with concern for its safety, my husband said, "It's just a frog." So, who's opinion was right? Each one of us had our own feelings and opinions on the situation. And for each one of us it was our experience viewed through our own looking glass. As for the frog, what about his viewpoint? Was he trying to follow me into the house? Was he looking for a place to stay? Or maybe he was showing me a way to be compassionate. All the while, he got crushed in my slider! My daughter was standing there just sobbing. Will he live? I'm thinking to myself, I don't know, but had to do something. She carried the frog outside. I showed her where to place him in a safe place. She was not convinced that he would live. I decided to do something to help this little fella. But that would mean I had to get close to him. Maybe even touch him. Yuck! I would do anything for my daughter. So, we got close to him, placed our hands over him, and just started praying. We asked God and the Angles to heal him. We agreed that when we came back in 30 minutes, if he was still there, we would bury him. If not, we knew God had listened to our prayers and healed him. We finished our prayer for him and walked away. I kept the dogs inside the house so they would not bother him.

Knowing that Freckles and Tigger would get anything that came through the yard. I once watched Tigger catch a bird in midair and they were always bringing dead animals as presents to me. Thirty minutes later, my daughter came running to me in the kitchen. Mom, come look! I thought to myself Oh boy, this could go either way. So, I stopped what I was doing, and we ran down the stairs to where we had laid the frog. I hesitated to think if he was still there. You will be happy to know that our frog friend is gone!! He lived; our prayers were answered! Thank you, Jesus! With such joy, we had a happy house again.

This frog, indeed, had a message for me. What I found out is that the Universe is always speaking to us. I learned that nature sends us messages through messengers. The Spiritual meaning of the frog is purification and renewal. The spiritual energy of the frog encourages us to cleanse our minds, bodies, and souls. There is a message here of transformation, communication, and good luck. Boy was that the message I needed to hear at that time. I just didn't know it.

There are many situations in our lives where we experience it one way, and other person or people experience it another. Back to the original question, is it right or wrong? Chocolate or Vanilla? In the situation above, was it right for me to be so scared of a frog? A harmless frog. Well, that is how I felt, scared. This was my emotion, a sense of fear. I was out of alignment. So yes, it was right for me because it matched that vibration at that moment. My husband laughed; he was in alignment. As for our daughter, who was also in alignment looked through the vibration of love. Through her looking glass of love, vibrationally, she helped that frog live another day. Our emotions are valid. We can never tell another that their emotions are wrong. We need to feel our emotions.

I'm sure there are many situations in your life that when you look back and think, I could have handled that better or much differently. Honestly, you handled it just perfectly at the time that you did. You see, we are always in the right place at the right time, doing the right thing. We learn from each experience and each other. That is this game called life. You want to find what works for you. Really that is where the terms chocolate and vanilla came from. Instead of always disagreeing with everyone in my life, because I usually did, being told I was wrong or even telling the other they were wrong. I decided to diffuse the discussion with that term, chocolate and vanilla. I'm a foodie, and

I relate everything to food. That is the one thing that everyone in the world could understand. We all eat, and we all have our own flavors we like. Whether it be salty, sweet, or healthy. We can all relate to food.

I started to notice people more intently. I wanted to understand what made them tick. I would find and use a term that they could understand. I would get a strange look as to what that even means. What does meat and fish have to do with our conversation? I even talked about what they did for a living. As to find some common ground. I tried many different alternatives, but chocolate and vanilla really stuck. At first, everyone thought they knew what it was. It was sweet. Are you calling me sweet? Then I would explain, and it really did diffuse the conversation. It helped me realize that just because someone did something differently doesn't mean I have to or even agree with them. Most of all, it doesn't mean it's right or wrong. I said this term so often that it was so natural to me. Each time I said it, I would have a different reaction. Some good, some crazy and some rejected me. Some thought I was saying black and white. I listened more to my conversations and the people I conversed with. I listened more intently to their reaction and their inflections in their voices along with their body language. I think it is important to communicate with clarity.

People are going to say and believe what they want. The trick is for you to believe what's best for yourself. Don't believe what others are saying about you.

# CHAPTER 5

## How Can We Be of Service to Others

I have been in the service business for most of my life, and I dealt with a lot of personalities. And somehow, I always found it fulfilling.

As far back as I can remember, I would help others in any way that I could. In school I would always offer to help the teacher in church or even at my grandparents' house. Of course, when I was young, I was told to help. I never had a choice. Still, I knew helping someone was a good thing. What I didn't know was that it was going to be a way of life for me.

In 2008, I developed a business, At Your Service with Style, LLC. I supplied staffing for private events in homes and at different types of public venues. In the beginning, I was a one-woman show. Soon realizing I could have more business with more servers. So, a dear friend of mine offered to help, and we became partners. She was someone who was always serving the Lord. She and her husband helped more people than I could count. They are really special people. I am blessed to have them in my life.

We jumped into it and started booking more events, which in turn needed more staff. Our business grew quite quickly. With more business came more stress. Even though we interviewed each person and knew who they were, I would see them act differently at each event. Not knowing what I know now, I would be a bit bossy and sometimes too much. I worked hard for the success of our business and had a certain reputation to uphold. Of course, I wanted everything done my way. Not realizing that different personalities do things differently. We could do the same job, just going about it differently and having the same results. I had a really hard time getting that down. I still wanted it done the way I was teaching. I could only see it through my eyes, and of course, it was my business. For a while, it all went well, and our business was very successful. We had our core team, who was with me even before we had an official LLC. They stayed through thick and thin. Then, there were others who did not like me and my attitude. They didn't know that I was a perfectionist and things had to be done the way I wanted them. My friend and partner worked on the business side while I was out in the field, working at parties. Here is where I really started to learn that there are always two sides to every coin. I just wanted to always be the head. If you know what I mean. Kinda one-sided if you ask me. Back then, it didn't matter. I took charge. My friend, who also took charge, helped me to see the light.

We continued for many years then the time came when my partner gave me back the business. I in turn, had given the partnership over to my daughter. She was young and not eager to serve. So, I continued booking and working with my staff. Doing what I knew best. At some point, this was my only income. I started to be stressed and a bit crazier than normal, shall we say. Some of my staff dropped off, and as you can imagine, so did business. The business I did have was great, and everyone loved our service. It was like two businesses in one. We served, and we cleaned. It just wasn't enough to survive. I would take on many things like dog, cat, and house sitting. We were just getting by. I was constantly asked if I do regular house cleaning. Now, this was not something I was remotely interested in. But in 2015, I added this service to our list, along with my regular service staff, which included, but was not limited to waitresses, bartenders, maître d's, cooks, and valet services.

The thought of adding cleaning houses was a bit overwhelming. I started small with some friends, and then the list grew. I guess I did a really good job because the word spread, and job after job was booked. So here I was, a one-woman show again but I quickly did what I did before. I added to the team. Some of the service team jumped on board with the cleaning. My business grew quickly. I had residential and commercial cleaning added to the list. I had over 45 independent workers. We cleaned many houses and offices. Things were going quite nicely. I found cleaning to be an interesting process.

I was in many different homes seeing that not everyone lived the way I do. I guess you would say I was a bit naive. I really did think that everyone valued their home and lived in a clean manner. Boy, was I wrong!! Now, don't get me wrong. I know I was there to do a cleaning job. I just wasn't ready for some of the things I saw. Why would anyone use their floor as a trash can? Discarded papers, candy wrappers, dirty dishes, and used tissues, you name it, on the floor. Some were not too far from the trashcan that was sitting there in the corner. Dirty clothes are all over the floor, ok, not so bad. The sheets have not been changed for a month. If I told you about the bathroom and how they keep their toothbrushes and what was all over the sink, you would die, or maybe not. A lot of chocolate and vanilla here. If you know what I mean. I was on the outside looking in, and the client was on the inside looking out. It was their dirt, so it didn't bother them. It really is all in how you look at it. A perspective from both sides.

Business was good. To this point, I was able to have extra, and I could help others. Although I always helped where I could. I was guided to give more and help more people. Remember, earlier in the book, we talked about a good friend. One who you tell everything to and is always there to listen. I had a good friend like that. We met in a spa that I was managing at the time. I also did this while building my business. We became fast friends. We like the holistic lifestyle and have many similar interests. She is a good person, and we talked all the time. Well, she was my go-to, but what I didn't realize was how much she was helping me. She would listen to me and then try to guide me. I did help her also, but in a business sort of way. The owner of the spa was tough and expected things to go a certain way. I could relate to that. It was her business, and at one point, she wanted to let this lady go. But I didn't, and this was not my business. So, I wanted to do something to save my friend's job. I had shown the owner how valuable this woman was to her and her business, and by week's end, she still had a job. I never told her I saved her job. I guess about a year or so had gone by and this woman decided to make a move to another state. I was happy and sad at the same time for her. This was something she was called to do. So, I helped her where I could and wished her well.

Some time passed, and I also left the spa. So, what's with this story, Cheryl? This woman is an important factor in how this book came about. We continued to be friends and talk as usual. She was enjoying her life on the west coast and me on the east coast. All the time she was there, I moved probably 3-4 times. Again, all while building my business, but by that time, I was divorced and doing things on my own with my daughter. As time went on, she was in a spot where she either had to move or bring in a roommate.

This is where I jumped in and said I can help. I was already helping others, but this one was my close friend, and I wanted to help her like she did for me. I was in a real good place, spiritually, physically, and monetarily. So, I offered to be her roommate. Of course, she thought I was crazy. But I think she always knew that. If you're my friend, you know I'm crazy, and I do what makes me happy. I was in alignment and the answer just came to me. I blurted it out; I can be your roommate. So, I live far away. I can pay my way, and I will make my way down there when I can. Mostly, it would put her mind at ease, and she wouldn't have to move. After that, she was home on the East Coast for a week, visiting her family, and we met up for lunch. During lunch, we had a great time catching up. At one point, I put an envelope in front of her with some cash in it. She smiled and said, "What's this for?" I said, "For the apartment." She said, "What? Wait, you're serious about that?" I laughed and said, "Does it look like I'm serious about it?" We were both so excited! And moved forward with our deal. All the years we were friends she heard me always use the term chocolate and vanilla, probably to the point of being sick of it. But she knew what I meant by it. So, it worked. I made it to the West

Coast many times during the year we were roommates. She was a sweetheart. I mostly drove with my truck full of apartment stuff. I had an old red Lexus at that time. Driving anywhere from 19-23 hours one way each time by myself. On one trip, I had to stop every 1,000 miles because I had a leak in my oil tank. What a trip that was. At 2, 3 & 4 in the morning at gas stations with the undesirables all by myself. My Angels were working overtime on that trip. They were with me the whole way. I would drive straight through. One time, I decided to fly and take my daughter with me. She was about 23 years old. That was an experience all in itself. At that point in my life, my daughter wasn't very happy with me. I tried to make her happy. Taking her on trips and doing whatever I could for her to be happy. Learning all the time that I could only do so much. If you have ever heard the saying ...

*You can't get sick enough to make someone well enough, you can't get poor enough to make someone rich enough, and you can't get sad enough to make someone happy enough.*

They are true statements. I learned fast that I could not breathe for my daughter, eat, or think for her. Let alone have a good time for her. Not for anyone else either. With that being said, our trip was experienced quite differently. I love the apartment and where it was located. I had a great room, my own bathroom, and a walk-in closet. I bought a small cabinet and decided to just use an air mattress. The first couple of times I went there, I slept on the floor on a mat. It didn't matter to me. I was just happy to be there in the beautiful weather with my friend. Well, for my 23-year-old, it was a huge problem. Same room, different points of view. I was happy, and she wasn't. My friend and my daughter liked each other. Thank God!

So, she softened the blow. My friend made lots of plans for us that week to explore the area and have a good time. There was one day towards the end of our trip when we went to this secluded beach. She told us to bring water shoes because we had to wade through this marshy area and put our things in a float. We were a bit taken back at first, but remember the minefield.

We followed my friend and her friend. We had one of the best days. The water was gorgeous blue and warm, and the beach was perfect. What a day. We floated in the beautiful calm water, but not knowing something must have been bothering my friend. Going back to her car she was suddenly quiet with us. She was a bit short with me on the car ride back. I did what I always do and tried to lighten the energy. Tried to make her laugh, and changed the subject. But she didn't have any of it. Our ride was quiet for the last 20 minutes. As we were getting to the apartment. She said something to me about my carefree attitude. I think I blocked it out because all I could remember was saying Chocolate and Vanilla, and then she snapped at me.

F you! You and that dam Chocolate and Vanilla. It means nothing! It's stupid! Well, I wanted to say F you too! But I didn't. I was learning to keep my big mouth shut. And believe me, that was a challenge all in itself! My daughter was making sure of it, too. I did keep my mouth shut and so for the remainder of the trip. That warm, beautiful weather suddenly turned cold.

Let's examine this. My friend was out of alignment, and I was in alignment. We both were at the same beach with the same people in the same water with the same sun. Apparently, we experienced it *much* differently.

That was the last trip I took over there for some time. And every time I said Chocolate and Vanilla, it brought me to that negative place in time. I blamed myself for quite a while. Then I realized that her attitude was her choice, and my attitude was mine. We just chose differently, hence Chocolate and Vanilla. But still, I had a hard time using that term because I was belittled. I allowed someone else's vibration to affect my own. That experience changed me and the way I looked at things. I was hurt then I became sad.

Months went by and at that time, we didn't have virtual payments. I still sent my check. I let that scene play over and over again in my mind. I felt bad because we didn't talk after that. All the thinking did was bring more heartache and misery to me. You see what you think about what you bring about. Like attracts like. I felt worthless, and business started to decline. I thought it was the times, or maybe the pricing was too expensive. I had to give my friend 2 months' notice to leave the apartment. That just put fuel on the fire and made me sad. But I had to survive for myself.

I took one more trip over there, cleaned out the apartment, packed my car, and came home with my tail between my legs. I did, however, leave a very nice card thanking her and left money for the utilities. If she was to tell the story, I'm sure it would be a bit different. Because she will be telling it from her point of view. And this is my point about chocolate and vanilla. We experience life through our own filters. So, how you feel attracts more of the same into your experience. I never heard from her again. It's been years and I often think of her and only wish the best for her.

# CHAPTER 6

## Influenced by Other Viewpoints

Not talking about chocolate and vanilla was like not eating for me. And remember, I'm Italian and love to eat! That experience really made me sad. I loved my friend, and we were very close.

Every time I had a life-changing experience, I would work on myself. Somehow, I always knew to look inside. Even if I had a fight or got angry, which happened often in my family. I would go to sleep and wake up the next morning all cheery. Who would have guessed that that would have created a problem in my life? Not me! But it did. My siblings didn't like it if we had a fight, and the next morning, I was happy. My brother used to say to me I can't stand you. We had a knockdown drag-out fight last night, and you're happy this morning like nothing happened. WTF! Yes, that's me always looking on the bright side. I also used to say there is a silver lining in every grey cloud. I thought, well, it's a new day, and that was yesterday. Why bring it into today? I really didn't know that was such a thing until I started listening to Abraham Hicks. What an inspiration she is, or they are depending on how you look at it.

Years into my journey of healing, a friend of mine sent me an audio of someone called Abraham Hicks. I thought Abraham was a man. Little did I know it was a woman Ester Hicks who was channeling this, Abraham. Now, I know that sounds weird, especially if you haven't heard of or listened to her. If you started your journey of enlightenment, you may already understand that we are spirit living in a physical body. And we are here to have an experience and with those experiences comes lessons. Boy, are their lessons. I have experienced the same one for years. I did tell you I was a slow learner. That is only when it comes to me. We will talk more about lessons in future chapters.

When we are born, we come into a little body. We are all spirit, and that is what guides us. We are born into a family that we have a soul contract with. Our journey starts as soon as we are conceived. Once we are born into this world, our physical journey starts. As physical beings, we are new here, and we are taught by our parents. Some of us may only have one parent, some of us may be given away for adoption, and some may be orphans. Wherever we are, our journey starts. We are learning immediately. We learn if hungry, we cry, if we are tired, we cry. If we have a dirty diaper, we cry. Crying is our form of communication at this point in our little lives. Our journey continues, and we learn to communicate our needs with the language we are given. Some of it is by speech, some by sound, and some by sign language.

We use all our senses to learn how to communicate. Some of us are limited by our senses that we are born with. So, we utilize what we are given to learn. We are very observant, and we use our senses to absorb our surroundings. Everything around us is energy. We are vibrating beings that use energy, and this is another way for us to communicate. As babies, we use this energy to know if something or someone is good or bad. It is a sense of feeling or just knowing. If we like the energy around us, we are comfortable and at peace. Maybe sleeping or laughing. If the energy is harsh, we cry and are uncomfortable with a sense of fear.

How does this grown human know what to do with this brand-new baby human? It's instinctual and spiritually known through that little voice inside you. We are all connected, so Mom & Dad can feel the love and joy with this little being. All they want to do is make you happy and give you lots of love. They do this by nurturing this little being. Giving it love, food, clothing, entertainment, guidance and more. This little being is pure joy, love, and light! Perfect alignment with spirit. Anyone who is around a baby can feel this love. This little being is brought to its new home here on this earth. All homes are different, with different families. Some are clean and tidy; some are dirty and messy.

Some are full of joy and excitement, and others doom and gloom. Some are big, and some small. Some are wealthy, and some are poor. Where ever this little being goes is the perfect place for them to be. You see, we already chose to have this experience here on earth. With that, we already chose our parents, siblings, grandparents, family members, friends and all the others to be in our lives from birth to death. We have a contract with God. Wait, what? How can that be? I lost my child, my parents, my lover, my best friend. No way I would have never chosen to have this experience I am having now! Never! I am in such despair, and I am hurt. Why would I have chosen this?

When we are in the spirit world, we have a choice to come to this physical world. There are many souls who do not want to come here. This is a difficult world to navigate. Yet, there are so many others who are very excited to come and experience this beautiful physical world. You are one of those beautiful souls who chose to come and experience such beauty, joy, and love.

You see, before your loved one passed on or, as I like to say, transitioned to the other side. You were in love! You lived in and out of alignment, but you were in love. Depending on your lessons needing to be learned. Your life went in a certain direction. Whatever it was, you were on this journey with your beloved person. Something changed, maybe suddenly or maybe a very slow-moving situation. Now, this beloved person is gone. They left you. Why would I have chosen for this to happen? We are here to experience love, and before we get here, we are so excited to experience this physical love that we do not read the fine print.

Being a spirit in a physical body is very different from just being a spirit. Spirit is light, pure joy, and love. Our physical body is ego, tissue, blood, bones—a denseness. So now we have this spirit mixed into this physical body. Or this physical body mixed into our spirit. We are living in duality. Remember that beautiful baby, pure with love and light in this new body, learning to navigate. This baby doesn't know what you know as an adult. As babies, we are still pure spirit. Ego hasn't developed yet. Our ego develops around age 8, when the left brain—the critical brain—hence ego, develops. Then, the right brain (spirit) and left-brain (ego) start to mix together. Before that, we live in pure spirit.

Have you ever had an experience with a young child where they already knew the answer? 'Out of the mouths of babes,' as the saying goes. Your ego is in full bloom, and you've been conditioned your whole life. Now, as a parent you will be conditioning your baby to your way of life. You can only teach what you know. So, how you were raised comes into the picture now. You may like or dislike the way you grew up, and along the way in your journey, you have changed a lot of things. But somehow, this old conditioning comes back. You start to experience some of these old behaviors again. Probably because you are sleep deprived, not eating enough. Because you give all you have to taking care of your newborn baby. You forget about you and your needs. Your parent or caregiver did the same for you. Although each generation makes it easier and easier to do things. Just by the experience that was had, there is a new product or teaching developed. You have something your parents probably did not have when you were born. Remember, they did the best they could with what they had. So, we raise our child based on what we know, have, and what we are doing. We live our lives based on what we were told, how we were conditioned, and what we experienced.

Think about it: if you're happy, you do things one way, and if you're sad or angry, you do them another. It's really that simple. So why not just be happy all the time. Is that really possible? It is if we just stay in our own lane. You can only breathe for yourself, just like they say when you go on an airplane. Put your oxygen mask on yourself first, then you can help someone else.

If you want to be happy, you must think, do, and say things that make you happy. It sounds easy, right. The recipe for a happy life is to be happy!! When we know better, we can do better.

# CHAPTER 7

## Interpretation of A Viewpoint

Everything we do in life teaches us something. It's up to us to see the lesson and the value in it. When it comes to lessons, I was a slow learner. I repeated the lesson many times, for whatever reason, but once I learned it. I got it! I would be so excited to have mastered the lesson, only to turn around and learn another. For many years in my life the lessons were challenging and repetitive. I thought I was getting it. But I was missing an important ingredient, me! I am a kind, giving, cheerful, positive, and loving person. So why all the hard lessons. How was I attracting the negative vibrations? Let's start with my 23-year relationship with my husband of 17 years. Family and friends, our businesses, financial hardship, and the list goes on. I'm sure you have your own list of what your lessons are. But I kept asking why? Why all the hardship? I am a good person. What is happening here? What's with all the bad and ugly? I found out very quickly: if you do not want to know the answer to the question, do not ask it.

I asked, I had to ask the question, and pow! Right in the face, the lesson showed up. If I wanted the answer to the question, it would be right there in the middle of the lesson. In every experience, there was one common denominator. You guessed it! It was me, as are you in yours. Let's see, I looked for a solution all the time when something was not going right. I found that if I learned the lesson the solution came easily. But if I didn't get it or refused to look at it, the experience became more intense. I put resistance on myself. What I found out about resistance is that it made my lessons harder. I had to find a way to release the resistance. It's like trying to paddle your boat upstream against the current. That's resistance, but if you just put the oars in the boat and floated downstream, that's going with the flow.

In my early years, I had always been successful in my work endeavors. I worked hard and earned good money. Most of the time, I had three sources of income. You can say I did a lot of juggling. I did well in the love department, and I had a lot of friends. I thought my life was good. I just did what I wanted, when I wanted, and how I wanted, and I had all the resources to support me.

Growing up, I was told constantly that I was dumb. I never got it right. How could I survive on my own? It was drummed into me that I would need a man to support me. Because I would not be successful and couldn't manage my money. Of course, I was out to prove them all wrong. I was not dumb. I could do it. However, I was constantly told I could not do it. How can you be so stupid? I told you to do it this way. Why don't you ever listen to me? You are not good enough. And there it is. That is what happened to me. I took on someone else's viewpoint of myself for myself. What I learned is that people can only give you what they have on the inside.

I knew I was a smart person and could do anything I wanted, but they had all these rules. I don't like rules, it is a form of control for me. Someone was always trying to control me. So, I became a rule breaker and was always fighting for me and what I wanted. This fight became tiring and wore me down, to, after a while, I started to believe what they told me. I started to believe the lies. This is what conditioning is all about. It is a form of control.

Here is the part that is so important. It doesn't matter what someone else thinks, says, or does when it comes to me/you. It took me a long time to get that because I did care what someone thought or said about me. What I didn't realize was how it affected me. I thought differently, like they did. I became feelingless and just did what I was told. After all, what could I do? I was young. So, I tried my best to just follow along, but down deep inside, I had this yearning to be successful! I wanted to be free and live life the way I wanted.

I loved the way I felt when I was happy. I also loved it when people I loved were happy. My dad was always laughing. He had that contagious laugh, and you just couldn't help yourself but laugh. If you were in his company and you didn't have a smile on your face or laugh. He would be a trickster to make you laugh. For instance, if you were sitting with him having a cup of coffee watch out. He would stir his black coffee, take the back of the hot spoon, and place it on your hand. He would always get a rise out of you. This created many laughs.

Wherever my dad went, people were always laughing. Oh, if you went to a show with him, be warned. You know, back in the day, there were live performances. Well, he would interact with the performers, and somehow, your name would be the one mentioned. And all the attention would be on you! If you were on vacation with him it was constant laughing. Just remember never to get into an elevator with him. Unless you had your gas mask on. If you know what I mean. My dad had a way of just getting you to love who you are and enjoy your life.

Although my dad grew up wealthy, he had a lot of challenges with his family. He would always have a smile on his face. He had an older brother who, let's just say, the sun rose and set on him. Some would understand it described as the prodigal son. My dad was always being put down by his parents. You know, never good enough. He worked twice as hard and was successful, but his parents never recognized him for it. They would say things like, why can't you be more like your brother, and he was told his mother didn't love him. His brother was sent to Harvard while my dad worked in the family business. My dad also learned to achieve success on his own. While his brother was, I guess, a good word for him would be a gigolo, I'm so glad my dad stayed true to himself! He was a great man! He was honorable, encouraging, successful, and joyful. I would compare him to Santa Claus. Yes, that is a good picture of who my dad was. That should give you an idea of his character. I guess you would say my dad looked inside himself and looked up to God to guide him. Laughter was just a great way to break the ice with others and keep the energy light.

When we were growing up, we always had a vegetable garden. Remember, we are Italian and had to have the tomato plants in the yard. My dad was quite proud of his gardens. We grew up on Elm Place in Nutley, but during our high school years, we lived in a town called Little Falls, NJ. We had a beautiful house on a beautiful piece of property with a huge garden. His tomato plants were at least six feet tall. Just amazing, he did enjoy his garden. We had an array of veggies, and of course, we had black and white fig trees. These trees were massive. The reason I'm telling you this story is for a couple of reasons. One, because getting out into nature and putting your hands in the soil is for your benefit. It is a very healing activity. You can see the fruits of your labor, shall we say. He so enjoyed it. That was his way of staying in alignment. The other reason is he loved to grow hot peppers. Again, I think it is our heritage. What he enjoyed most about those hot peppers was fooling others with them. If you stepped foot into our house, no matter who you were, you were introduced to his hot peppers. He would say, do you like peppers? And if you answered yes, you were in for it. He would then take to you his garden out back. Come on, I want to show you something. Look at these peppers! I grew them myself. Would you like to taste one? Of course, he would get the occasional no, but somehow, everyone fell for this. He would grab one off the stem and say here, just take a bite. The person would say ah, aren't they hot? He would say no, they are not hot. Here, I will take the first bite. And he would take that bite and be fine. Well, of course, the other person changed their mind. Ok, I'll take a bite. Now, if you know anything about Italian hot peppers, the first bite is mild, and there aren't any seeds. The second bite and after is where all the heat is. Now you have people yelling my mouth is on fire and cursing him out. But my dad always had the loaf of Italian bread ready to give you after. You can imagine the laughs. Of course, it was more hilarious for him than the other person at first. People were able to laugh, but they never fell for the garden joke again.

I guess my dad's way of laughter gave him peace and happiness in his life. It helped him to forget about all the trauma that was in his past. I realize now as an adult he wanted to share this laughter with others. There is nothing too serious in life except death and taxes, he would say. He had an amazing spirit and was full of joy. I think that is where I learned to be happy. Just being happy is the best vibration to be on.

We all have feelings and emotions. We use these emotions to feel and navigate our way through life. Whether we are a child, teenager, or an adult, at any age, we have feelings. These feelings start with a thought then these thoughts turn into things. If you were put down or embarrassed when you were younger. You develop a sense of shame or perhaps guilt. This develops in the form of fear of not being good enough. Now, when you look at someone, you look through those feelings of guilt and shame. You see, at that time, I didn't know that the adults around who told me I was dumb really felt that way about themselves. They were just projecting it onto me.

We can never be sure of what is really going on inside someone's head. No matter how well we think we know them. You don't know what makes them tick. You don't know how they truly feel or what they think. They may tell you how they feel at that moment, but our emotions are inside of us and just for us. What I have found is that we influence others by how we feel. What we say and what we do. We can really help or hurt another person by the way we treat them.

I cannot speak for you, but for me, I have had that happen. I had my mind made up to do something, and then someone close to me would poo-poo it. So, what did I do? I changed my mind and listened to the other person. Remember, earlier in the book, I said I was constantly being told I was dumb. Well, I wanted to be a veterinarian. It was my dream when I was younger. I allowed other people's opinions of myself to affect me and what I wanted. With the constant thought in my head that I was dumb and not good enough, I started to believe what I was told, not realizing that it was their own thoughts about themselves being projected onto me. I believed it, and what you think about, you bring about. So, I believed that I was incapable of being a veterinarian.

People can only share what they know. They learn, do, and then teach. As a student, you must be ready to learn. What you want to be aware of is the vibration level the teacher is on. Let's face it: you can be given a lot of information, good or bad. Is that what's good for you. Because if you're a vegetarian and you are given meat, hmm, that is not going to work for you, is it? Another one of my favorite sayings is, "Don't yuck my yum!"

People can only give you what they have inside of themselves. It's impossible to share something you do not have. What I have learned is that we keep our bad experiences locked up inside of us. Wanting to throw away the key. What really happens is that these emotions sit at a cellular level in our bodies. And are always there lurking around. Somewhat stagnant until triggered. These trigger points bring up these old feelings from our past. What we do with them is the key to our happiness.

We can choose to fire on the old feelings at the person or people who triggered us. The old fear arises. This is where we would go into fight or flight. That cortisol level rises, and we are ready to do battle. How will this help us? It shows us where we can start to heal. In order for us to feel better we need to know what it is that's stored in our emotional system. You must know what you have stored in order to clean out.

Have you ever had a closet full of stuff? You just kept adding stuff to it. Until finally it was so full you couldn't add another thing. Do you know what is in there? How long has it been there? The only way to have a clean closet is to unload it. You decide today is the day. I am cleaning out that closet. You walk into the room where the full closet is. You look around and say, where will I put all of that stuff to go through it? How can I do this now? You get overwhelmed and just forget it. You walk away and leave it for another day. Our feelings are a lot like that closet. We just stuff them away. We had a bad feeling and didn't want to feel it, so we stuffed it down. Maybe we just covered it with food, alcohol, sex, drugs, or even shopping. We stifled our feelings because it was uncomfortable to feel. What we do instead is try to numb the feeling of despair, fear, shame, and unworthiness. We find a way out. It hurts too much to feel like this. I need to find a way to live my life. This is where addiction finds its way into our daily life.

# CHAPTER 8

## How Do You Feel About It?

Why would you eat something that makes you sick? Why would you eat something that you love but you know will make you sick?

Eating something that makes you sick is like taking on someone else's judgment or criticism, even fear. Have you ever been in the company of a person who is angry or throwing a fit? I have, and it makes me feel sick. I do not like the vibration it holds. Perhaps in the office this has happened to you. The work is piling up, and there don't seem to be enough hours in your day to complete it. Perhaps there have been layoffs, and you have doubled the workload. You can only do so much with the time you have, but your boss doesn't care; he wants it done. After all, his boss is coming down on him/her. People are panicking with lots of stress all around. You can't help but feel this stress, and it makes you feel uneasy, eventually sick. Here is where I would use my crystals or essential oils to help me feel better. I had to find something to make me happy and not to feel the stress in the office. We will talk about that in a later chapter.

Eating something you love but you know you will pay for it later. This is like a family member or close friend. You love them, you really do! It's just that after you spend time with them, you are drained. Kind of like feeling sick. You may love ice cream and be lactose intolerant. You know what happens to you if you eat the ice cream you love. Why torture yourself? I bet you can find an ice cream that has ingredients you can enjoy without the fallout. Not as easy with a family member. But you can spend less time with them. Spend more time on yourself finding ways to be happy. Your happiness comes first.

If this is the case with the job. Sounds like it is time to find a new one. One you enjoy, you can get your work done. Where you like your boss and the people in your office. When you enjoy the work you do, you are much happier. When you are happy you are on a higher vibration. That's great. Finding a new job is much easier than finding a new family member or even a good friend. You may be surprised it is easier than you think!

As we learn who we are, our interests change. Remember, being in and out of alignment changes the lens through which we view things. Life really is all about how you look at it. Knowing the difference between being happy and sad, rich and poor, loving or hating.

My question is .... Why would anyone waste their precious time here doing anything else but living a happy, loving, joyful life? I know we have to experience the good, bad, and the ugly to know what it is that we want. But do we need to spend so much time in the negative?

It just doesn't make sense to me. So, I tried it. I tried to be happy and put on those rose-colored glasses. Of course, I was told you're not normal. You're not living in reality. How can you be so happy all the time? Truth be told, I wasn't happy all the time. I tried eating the food I really loved that made me sick. When that happened, I took a nap or went to sleep. I woke up in a new vibration. By going to sleep, the resistance is released.

If I offered you ice cream or an apple, which would you choose? What is your belief process on the subject? Which one would make you smile? Quick story to share on this exact subject. When my daughter was born, I chose to raise her in a holistic fashion. She was in cloth diapers. I made all her food from scratch, all organic of course. Back then, 31 years ago that is, everyone thought I was nuts. Organic was not as mainstream as it is now. Family members could not understand why I did what I did. At the age of 7, she attended a birthday party. You know the fun and games type of place where they served pizza and ice cream. At this party, there may have been 25-30 kids. All of us moms were chatting, and the kids were eating. As we always do. When it was time for dessert, they put the ice cream out in front of each child. It was all vanilla unless a child asked for chocolate. When they put this ice cream in front of my daughter. She politely pushed it and said, no thank you. The nice waitress bent down and said Ok, would you like chocolate? She said, no thank you. Do you have an apple? Remember, we are Italian, and we are not quiet people. So, everyone heard her ask for this apple. At that moment, I heard whose child is this? With all eyes on me I said proudly mine! You would have thought my daughter asked for a filet mignon or something. There was such a fuss. *An apple, no ice cream, what are you doing to this child? Can't she have ice cream? You crazy health nut! Of course, she can have ice cream! As much of it as she wants.* I taught my daughter to choose what is best for herself and what she likes, not what others like for her. She did just that. She chose an apple. Fast forward to today she knows how to choose for her life. What to eat, what to wear, where to go, and who to hang around with. She gets to choose to be happy. And this is the point I am trying to make.

You get to choose! You get to choose everything in your life, and it is full of choices. It's like a buffet with everything you could imagine. Yet you are not going to eat it all at once. You are going to take a little of this and a little of that and put it on your plate. Taste it, and if you like it, you can go back for more. You wouldn't go back for more of something you didn't like. Would you eat it because your friend wanted you to eat it, even if you didn't enjoy it? What if that very friend made fun of you for your food choices. Would you let it affect you? Nope, you would probably just let it roll off your back.

# CHAPTER 9

## How to Stay in Alignment

We all go in and out of alignment. If you are a human, most likely, it happens every day. Do you know how to go back into alignment when you fall out? Earlier in the book, I used the term, stay in your own lane. I want to use this as an example for alignment. If you do not know what alignment is, this example may help.

Think of a three-lane highway, and you are driving in one of those lanes. If you do not drive, you can be a passenger or even take the bus. First, we need to drive onto the highway. Using the acceleration lane, we gradually merge into the fast-moving traffic. Once you are on the highway, choose a lane. Staying in your lane of choice, you are in alignment with the road. Cruising along, listening to your tunes. Feeling joyful and confident. You are in control of your vehicle. Staying in your lane. This is like being in alignment with your body. Traffic starts to build up, and you're still bouncing to your music. You feel good. No concern for what is happening in any other lane but your own. The traffic doesn't bother you because you feel good. You get to your destination on time. All is well in your world.

Take that same scenario, but now someone jumps in your lane, cutting you off. It startles you and throws you off your game. Jamming on your brakes, maybe swerving a bit. What kind of mood does that put you in? Cursing at the knucklehead pressing on your horn, probably trying to drive up next to him so he can see how mad you are. Probably a few other thoughts or choice words. So, what now? You were so happy, just enjoying your time staying in your lane, in alignment. This just threw you out of alignment. It scared you, thoughts of an accident occurring. How you handle this will determine how the rest of your day will go.

If you were in a bad mood when you started out, chances are this would have made you even more mad. That traffic starts to really annoy you. You are going to be late for your destination. Now you want to scream at the world.

If you were in a happy mood, you might have still felt the fear of an accident, but you were able to shake it off because you were happy to begin with. We have choices in life. How we choose to react to a situation will determine where we go. Like attracts like.

It's not about what you say but how you feel. When you're in alignment, you are in tune with your inner being. This is the spiritual part of us. When you are out of alignment, you are in tune with your ego. This is the physical part of us.

The ego wants you to listen to it. It wants you to live in fear, regret, anger. It wants you to wallow in self-pity and to look for validation outside of who you really are. Always trying to prove who you are. It wants you to work hard for everything, keeping you in poverty.

Spirit is pure, unconditional love. Spirit is light and full of joy. Spirit is God, source, creator, our inner being. Spirit never dies and never needs proof. Spirit is abundant.

When we tune into our inner being, we are in alignment. When we live through our ego, we are out of alignment. Sounds simple, just like the lanes on the highway. You are either in your lane or someone else's. Life is much more enjoyable when you stay in your own lane. After all, we can only control what we think, say, feel, and do. If you want a happy life, it starts with a thought. Think happy thoughts, and you will create a happy feeling. When you feel happy, you attract happiness. It's about how you feel. So simple yet so challenging for us.

I choose to live a happy life. I am happy, healthy, wealthy, and wise. This is an affirmation I use daily, along with so many others that are listed in the back of this book.

If it is so easy to be happy, why is it that there are so many sad people in this world? So many people suffer from anxiety, depression, and poverty. They live in fear and doubt and worry. What is it about our society that causes this sadness? There are a lot of happy and successful people too, living in the same environment—two ends of the spectrum. We are here to experience this beautiful, abundant earth. Each one of us has a purpose with God-given talents. Do some of us have instructions, and others do not? The thing is, we take directions from our parents and caregivers, who in turn learned from their parents. We learn what we live through our environment. And until we learn something different or better we don't know any better.

We start out learning in school at an early age the basics of reading, math, and history. I don't think they teach writing in school anymore. I went to a Catholic school, so you better believe I learned how to write. At school, we learned how to get along with others. We had teachers to communicate with, and most importantly, we developed our friendships. Some of which last a lifetime. Besides our home environment, we have added school and sports. So many personalities to deal with. Many highs and lows. If you were lucky enough, you would find a good group of kids to be your friends. If not, there was that bully who paid you a visit. We had many experiences with others. We digested these behaviors and mixed them with what we knew at that time. After that, subconsciously, we mixed the learned behaviors and made them our own. We took what we learned at school and brought it home to our family.

Talking about our experiences and asking questions may hide our true feelings. Here, we were told how to act and what to say. Each household had a different vibration, corresponding to a different type of education. This is good; this is bad—another experience in which we were conditioned to believe what someone else thought to be true. You can make anything in your experience true or false; it's all in your belief system. Continually repeating and visualizing can make it so. Let's look at another example of conditioning.

The story of the eagle and the duck. As a baby, the eagle was saved and placed with a flock of ducklings. There was one of him and numerous ducklings. This eagle grew big and strong with beautiful wings, noticing that he was different from his siblings. He was just happy and kept pecking along with the flock.

One day, two eagles were soaring above the flock and noticed him. They landed next to him and said, "Why do you spend your time with this flock of ducks?" Confused, the eagle said, "I am a duck, and this is my family." The other two said, "Look at us. Do we look like you?" "Why, yes, you do." "Do the others look like us?" "No, they don't." "Look at your wings and spread them out. You can fly high above in the sky. You were made to soar high!"

Still confused, but with the help of the other eagles, he decided to try. At first, he could not do it. It was unusual to him. Nothing he had ever tried before. He said, "I can't do this thing you speak of." The others coached him and told him he could do it. "Just try again and again until you are flying. Flying is as natural to you as swimming in the pond is to the duck."

So, the eagle on the ground tried once, then twice, and the third time, he took off into the sky. With the help of his new flock, he could fly, something he never knew was possible. He was so proud of himself. "Look at me; I am flying!"

You see, we become what we live. That eagle was conditioned to his environment. Changing the way he lived, he thought he was a duck. He was conditioned, and he believed.

What has your conditioning done for you? Are you a duck or an Eagle? Are you content with where and how you live, along with who you are? Do you have dreams? Have you fulfilled them? Do you even know what is possible for you? Just like the eagle who didn't know who he was, it was inside him all the time, his true nature. His authentic self. Yet he was conditioned by his environment to believe he was a duck.

Your true self is waiting to come out!

Our focus is an important factor in our lives. What we focus on, we attract. This next thing is something I share during my seminars.

I want you to take a piece of paper and draw a line down the middle. Next, on the left side of the paper number it 1-10. Starting with number 1, write the word positive. Continue with the word positive down to number 9. Then, at number 10, write the word negative. On the right side of the paper, start with the word negative and continue to number 9. Then, at number 10, write the word positive. It should look something like this.

| | |
|---|---|
| 1. Positive | 1. Negative |
| 2. Positive | 2. Negative |
| 3. Positive | 3. Negative |
| 4. Positive | 4. Negative |
| 5. Positive | 5. Negative |
| 6. Positive | 6. Negative |
| 7. Positive | 7. Negative |
| 8. Positive | 8. Negative |
| 9. Positive | 9. Negative |
| 10. *Negative* | 10. *Positive* |

You can be living a life like column one. All is going well, but you have that one negative thing happening. Instead of focusing on all the good in your life, you focus on the one bad thing. By focusing on that one negative thing, you change all the positive to negative.

You can be living a life like column two. All is going bad for you, but you have that one good thing happening. You start focusing on that one positive thing in your life. By focusing on that one positive thing, you change all the negative to positive.

Appreciate who you are, your health, all you have, all the people in your life. All is well in your world!

# CHAPTER 10

## Who Are You?

You are spirit living in a physical body along with this ego. We live in a state of polarity and duality.

Polarity, as stated in the dictionary, is the quality or condition inherent in a body that exhibits opposite properties or powers in opposite parts or directions, or exhibits contrasting properties or powers. It refers to the particular state, either positive or negative, with reference to the two poles or electrification.

Duality, as stated in the dictionary, is the quality or state of having two different or opposite parts or elements. Dualism refers to a difference between two opposite things.

Our spirit is a form of electricity—a vibration and energy. Our bodies are made of bones, blood, and cells; it's physical. Some of us choose only the physical part of who we are, kind of like the eagle living with the ducks. Others, however, choose to look inside and explore the spiritual part of us—like the soaring part of the eagle. Either way, it's all good as long as you are living a happy life. The eagle thought he was living a happy life; he just didn't know how much better it could be—until he was shown who he truly was. Sometimes in life, all we need is a leg up.

When my clients come to me with situations they are usually looking for some answers. My job is not to give them the answer because what is good for me is not necessarily good for them. I know my flavor, and they are looking for theirs. My job is to help them see what is already inside of them. Their answers have been there all along. They have just been covered up by the conditions they are living in.

When we understand who we are, we start to attract new conditions. When you ask, it is given. We usually don't pay attention to the answer. Because we still have our clouded thinking. If you are reading this book, you are probably looking for some answers. That is where I was 20 years ago. Looking for some answers. I asked many questions, and the answers were given to me. I just couldn't see it. I started my journey looking for all those answers. What I found is that all I had to do was look inside of me. A lot easier said than done. How can I do this? I am so busy, always working, making a living, supporting myself and my daughter. I don't have time. I also learned that if I didn't find time to look inside myself to live a happy life. I would depend on others to make me happy, and then I would only be living their happiness, not mine. Then that would make me unhappy.

I started by keeping myself healthy. I am a stress eater. Something I learned about myself through my journey. As I stated earlier in the book, I lived a holistic lifestyle, but that doesn't mean I didn't eat sugar, chips, or drink wine. When I was stressed, I would eat chocolate and chips and have a glass of wine. I was eating and drinking my feelings away. So, I thought. I learned quickly that it only made it worse. I gained weight and was more depressed. Then I got mad because I was asking questions to better myself. How did I end up here? The answer to my question was to tune into who I am. Stop covering yourself up with all this weight. My process had begun I just didn't know it. As I continued to read self-help books I would be guided to try different things to help. God always puts the right people in your path. He did put someone there who helped me with my physical journey. He had been a personal trainer in the past. We dated for a while, and he guided me to start with my food intake. Then, he encouraged me to start running. Running?!! Are you crazy! I can just about walk up the stairs. With his guidance, help, and encouragement, I started. I had to walk first before I could run. I had to first condition and prime my body. He started me on a protein shake schedule. Then had me walking every day, no matter what the weather conditions were. One day, he had me meet him at a school in the middle of the day. He said bring your sneakers. I thought that was an interesting place for a date. I should have realized when he said sneakers. We met, and he walked me over to the track. In all my 46 years of life, I had never placed one foot on a track. Again, are you crazy? I was annoyed and started to walk away. He said if you never try, you will never know. I will be with you every step of the way. Huffing and puffing, I tried. I ran, then I walked, I ran again and walked again. Before I knew it, I made one lap around without stopping. Because of his encouragement and faith in me I was able to do it. Sometimes, we need others to hold faith for us, in us, until we can believe in ourselves. After that, I ran at ungodly times in the morning and after work. It was amazing. I was so happy and proud of myself. One day, he came to me and said I signed you up for a race. A what?! Yes, a race, a 5K race. This man was nuts. But again, he had faith in me, and I believed what he told me. I did my very first race and came in at 36 minutes—

not the fastest, not the slowest, but my best. I had accomplished something that was outside of my wheelhouse. I tried something new. After all, you don't know what you don't know. From that time on, I ran three races a year for about three years. I loved it.

From that experience I learned to eat what was best for my body and exercise. It did help me, but there was still a matter of these unfelt emotions from my childhood. Remember what he said, "You don't know unless you try." You guessed it, I tried other things. I would get massages and go to the chiropractor. I tried kinesiology, acupuncture, and meditation, all of which worked if I continued to go. Because of the time and cost involved, I looked for other available options. I was always drawn to holistic medicine and used essential oils. I was really attracted to the oils and found someone who knew a lot about them.

I educated myself through her teachings. I applied, ingested, and diffused these beautiful essential oils. I just loved them! I loved the way they made me feel! So,

I started my journey with Young Living Essential Oils. This information is listed in the back of the book. It has been over 13 years since then, and I still love the way I feel and smell because of these beautiful oils. And as my friend and mentor Suzanne would say, there's an oil for that!

I also learned a lot about crystals and what they do for me and my health. Some would say crystals are just rocks. I have been told I have rocks in my head. I wear rocks on my wrist and my neck!! The use of crystals I learned from my dear friend I worked with at the spa. You learned about our journey earlier in the book. I was so amazed by her knowledge of these beautiful stones and their value. She did a healing session for me and did this thing called Reiki along with crystals placed all around me and on my body. Woah, was that powerful. That was the best I had felt in years. I got more involved in crystal healing. Another love of mine! I learned about Reiki. Had many sessions, then learned it myself. There are so many modalities to aid us in our journeys. You just have to find what works for you.

What I found from all this learning, training, and doing is that it all starts with a mindset. You really can be, do, or have anything that you want. Almost anything can help you, Bemer, oils, crystals, reiki, reading, diet. It is in your belief that it will work. Your mind is powerful, and when you align it with your emotions and your faith, you have the winning recipe for a happy life.

It really is.... All about Alignment!

**The bird on the branch does not put its trust in the branch. It puts its trust in its wings.**

## Affirmations:

* I am happy, healthy, wealthy, and wise.
* I am love, I give love, and I receive love.
* I love and appreciate myself.
* I love and forgive myself.
* I am sorry. Please forgive me. Thank you. I love you.
* I am enough.
* I give enough.
* I receive enough.
* I have enough.
* I am strong.
* I am powerful.
* I am who I am, and that is enough.
* I live in a vibrant, healthy, fit, and sexy body.
* Everything is always working out for me.
* All is well in my world.
* Out of this situation, only good will come.

* I accept good graciously into my life. All my needs and wants are met abundantly now and always.

* I instruct my subconscious mind to only follow my higher self, in spite of what my mind says.

* I love and appreciate money for helping me live such an awesome life.

* I am a money magnet.

* Money comes to me easily and effortlessly from all directions, expected and unexpected.

* In my world, nothing ever goes wrong.

* I am more than what bothers me. I am more than my troubles.

* Light, joy, and peace abide in me. My sinlessness is guaranteed by God.

* Perfect health is my divine right, and I claim it now.

* I am divinely guided and protected at all times.

* I release all negative things about my past and all worries about my future.

* I forgive you completely, and I free you from our past. I only wish the best for you.
* Divine plan.
* Divine order.
* Divine guidance.
* Divine timing.

My life is one of abundance; an abundance of joy, love, and blessings, and free of any worry. I help grow this abundance to make the world a better place.

# ABOUT THE AUTHOR

Cheryl has a diverse background in retail, restaurants, catering, holistic living, and mediumship. She owns two businesses, At Your Service with Style LLC and Butterfly Wellness LLC. Although in some shape or form, she has always been in service helping others. From a small child, she has always been able to communicate with the spirit world and has listened to her guidance. Today, through spirit, she has written this book on being happy and believes it is all about our connection on the inside through God.

It's all about Alignment!

# REFERENCES

Butterfly Wellness, LLC, Butterflycs09@gmail.com

At your Service with Style, LLC, -

Cherylgillespie@rocketmail.com

Bemer IBD#US45038
https://2Feelgood.bemergroup.com

Young Living Essentials Oils,
https://www.youngliving.com/us/en/referral/143881
z

Louise Hay, you can heal your life

Wayne Dyer, the Shift

Ester and Jerry Hicks, Ask and it is given

Sonia Choquette, Trust your Vibe

www.ingramcontent.com/pod-product-compliance
Lightning Source LLC
Chambersburg PA
CBHW051539120626
46551CB00013B/1290